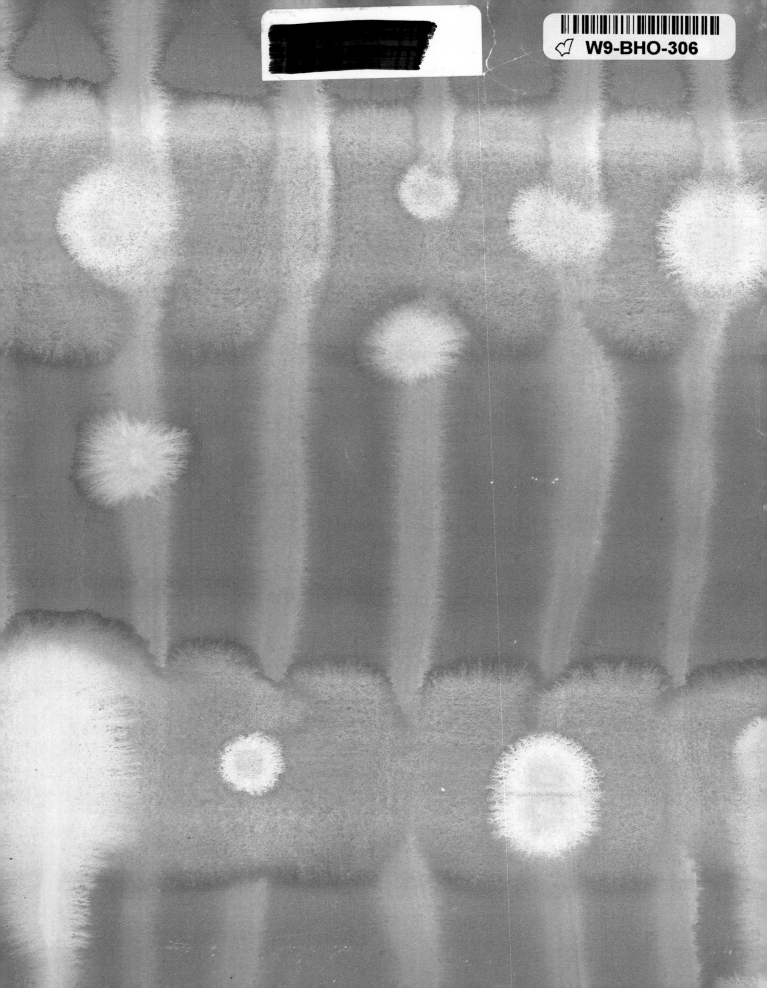

ANTARCTICA

HELEN COWCHER

Farrar, Straus and Giroux
New York

In the cold far south, in Antarctica,
live emperor penguins, Weddell seals,
and Adélie penguins.

The emperor penguin lays her egg in winter, when it is dark both day and night. Then she leaves to feed at sea. While she is gone, her mate carefully nestles the egg on top of his feet for two months.

He huddles in a tight circle with his friends, against the freezing winter storms.

Meanwhile, his mate is feeding at sea

. . .where danger lurks.

A ferocious leopard seal!

Luck is with the emperor this time.
She leaves the water safely and trudges
back to the rookery.

There is great excitement because their chick has just hatched.

But the male emperor is hungry and
weak. It is his turn to go to sea to find
food.

When it is spring, the sun at last
shines again in the Antarctic sky.
A Weddell seal climbs onto the ice
to have her pup.

The Adélie penguins have also come onto the ice. On their long journey to the rocky shore, where they will lay their eggs, they pass the emperor chicks.

The Adélies build their nests out of pebbles. They take turns keeping the eggs warm until the hatching.

Just beyond the nesting place, some
men have built a base camp.

Suddenly the Adélies hear
a terrible whirring noise:
helicopters! They panic and
leave their eggs unguarded.

Skuas swoop in to have a feast!

Frightened by the helicopters, the Adélies will not nest here again.

The emperors, too, are uneasy.
They have heard huge
explosions, and seen ice
and rock hurled high
into the air.

Out at sea, anxious songs ring out
from the depths. Weddell seals call to
their friends under the ice. Metal hulls
are pushing through the pack ice,
banging, crunching, booming nearer.

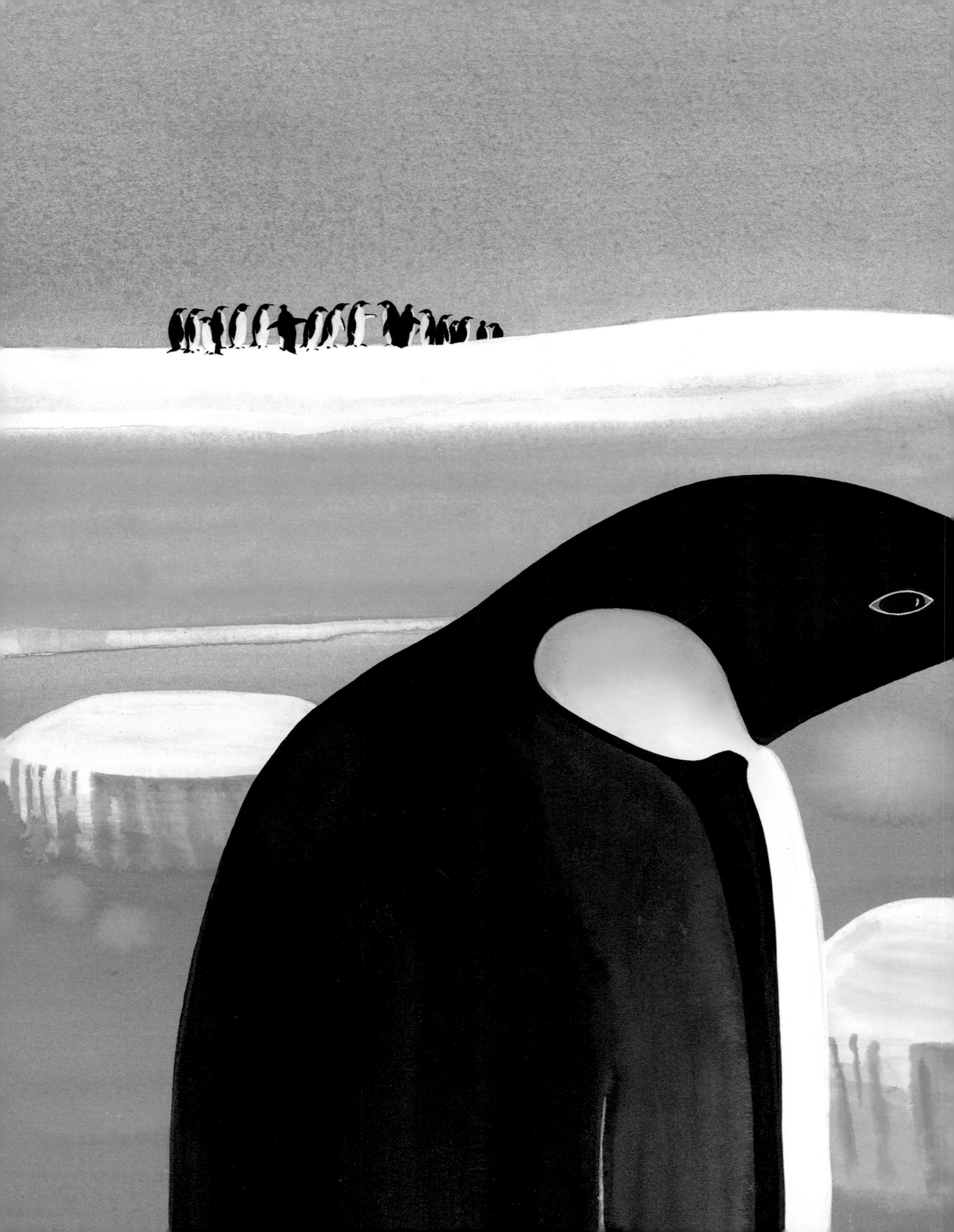

The penguins and the seals have always shared their world with ancient enemies, the skuas and the leopard seals. But these new arrivals are more dangerous. The seals and penguins cannot tell yet whether they will share or destroy their beautiful Antarctica . . .

E
COW   Cowcher, Helen.
           Antarctica.

$15.00   Grades 2-3   10/08/1997

DATE